The Black Plague Dark History
Children's Medieval History Books

BABY PROFESSOR
EDUCATION KIDS

Speedy Publishing LLC
40 E. Main St. #1156
Newark, DE 19711
www.speedypublishing.com

Copyright 2016

Have you heard of the terrible Black Death? Hello kids! Let's sing! Are you familiar with this nursery song?

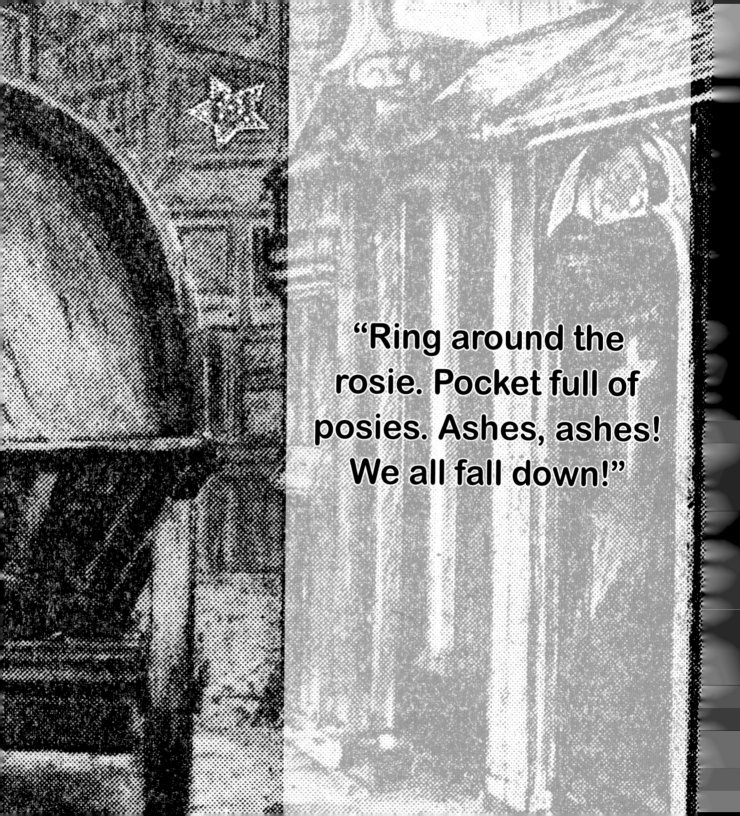

This song is related to the black plague that struck across Europe in the Middle Ages and caused the death of more than 20 million people there. Read further and discover how the Black Death relates to the song.

The Black Death is one of the tragic events in history. It is the deadly plague. It affected every part of Europe.

What is Black Death? It was one of the most horrible diseases during the 14 century in Medieval Europe. It was a deadly disease. The disastrous disease was caused by bites of fleas. The fleas normally lived on rats, but they would also live on humans. When they got the disease, the fleas infected people with their bites. The plague was a communicable disease. In other words, fleas could pass it to people, and people could pass it to other people.

How did it begin? It started in the 1200s. The disease was first felt in the Himalayan Mountains, between India and China. The plague traveled westward with rats who hid away in cargo, because the fleas on the rats carried the plague with them. These were black rats that thrived in European merchant ships and were carried to Europe.

Europe changed into a scary and horrible place because of the plague.

So many people died that some whole villages had no living people left. People were afraid to travel and at the same time afraid to stay home. One out of every four people died from the plague in Europe.

The people called
the disease "the
Great Mortality".
Some called it
"The Pestilence".

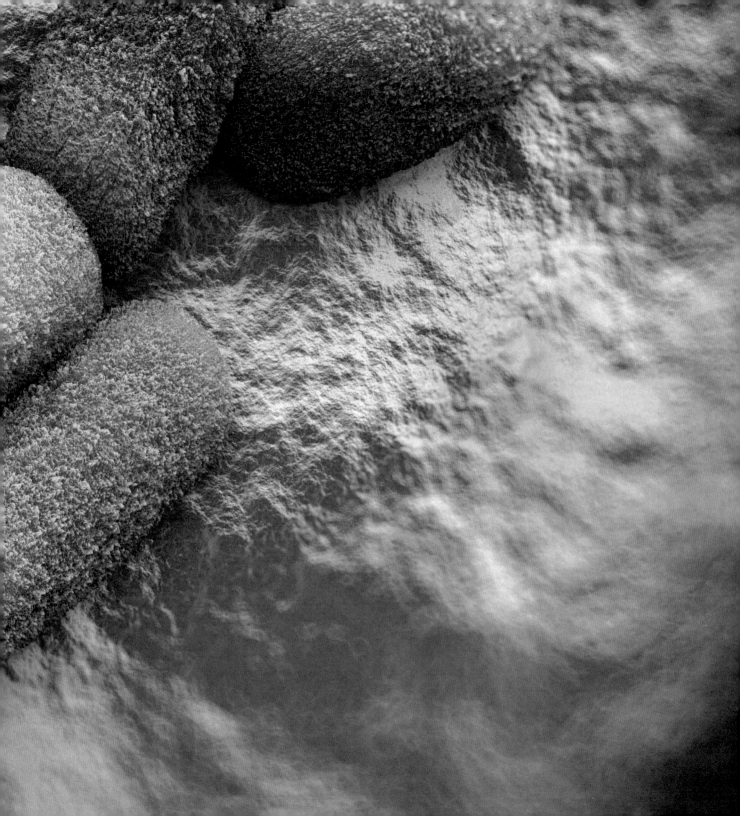

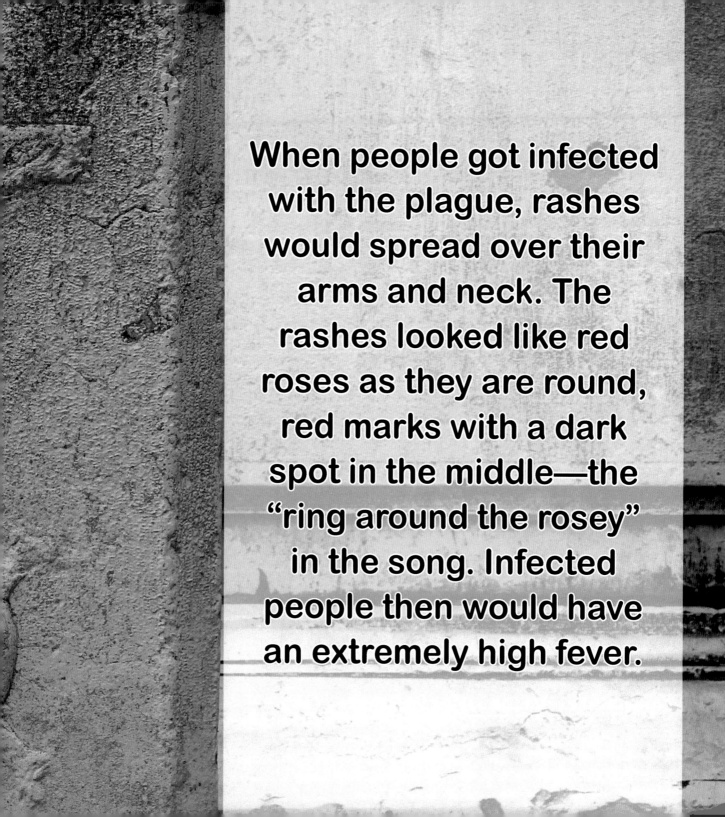

When people got infected with the plague, rashes would spread over their arms and neck. The rashes looked like red roses as they are round, red marks with a dark spot in the middle—the "ring around the rosey" in the song. Infected people then would have an extremely high fever.

They would fell unconscious and almost all of them would die within a few days. The disease was really disastrous! People would cover the dead and the dying with posies or fragrant flowers, and this is the source of the "pocket full of posies".

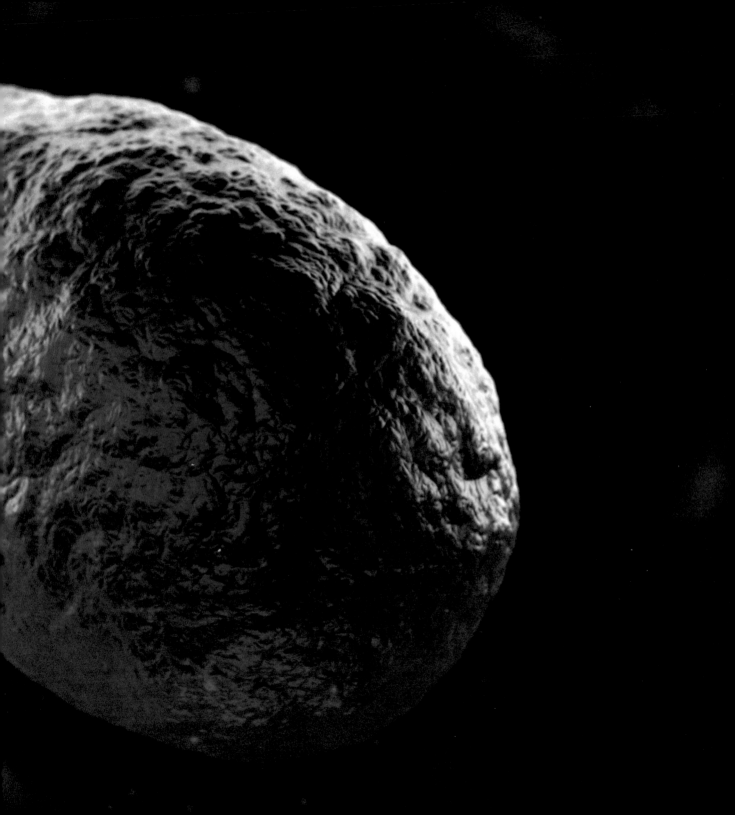

The houses of the infected people had to be burnt to prevent the spread of the disease, as the "ashes" in the song reminds us. Victims often just collapsed in the street: "we all fall down". The deadly disease spread to villages and cities and many people died.

Now, does that nursery rhyme sound different to you? Come on. Sing it again! Yes, definitely it's about the deadly plague that killed so many in Europe. It sort of feels funny to sing it in the playground, doesn't it?

The people in the Middle Ages thought that God was punishing them. They did not understand about germs, or that the rats were carrying them.

In 1348-49 the Black Death spread violently across England. The first signs were often swellings in the groin. These were referred to as buboes (swellings), from which we get the name Bubonic Plague. In September, 1348, the plague spread to London. There was no cure for the disease during this time.

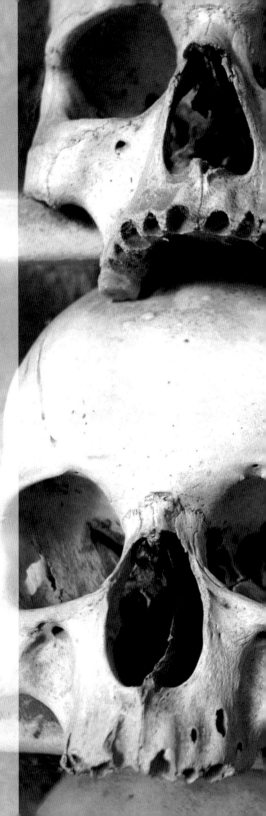

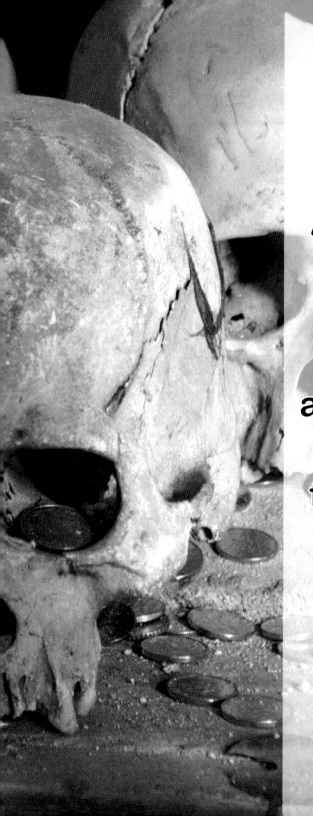

Alfonso XI of Castile was the only ruler who got infected of the deadly disease and died. Other kings and queens stayed far away from towns and cities where people were sick.

Did you know that the Back Death was only the second deadly disease of the Middle Ages? The first great sickness was known as Justinian's Plague. It occurred in the 6th century. Like the Black Death, Justinian's plague was also widespread and deadly.

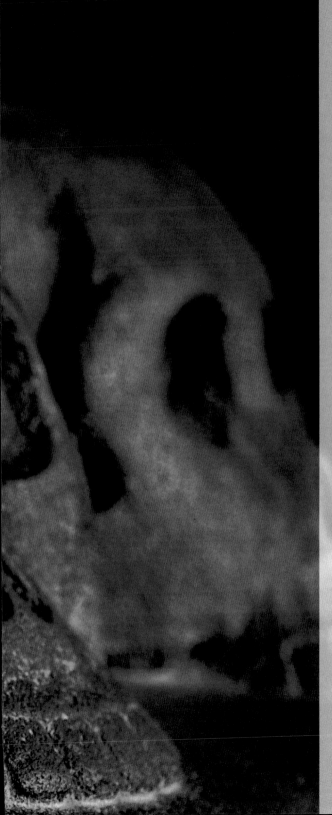

Scientists have concluded that the deadly plague was caused by Yersinia pestis, a bacteria carried by rat fleas. Rats were common in medieval homes, shops, and ships; and wherever they went, the fleas went with them.

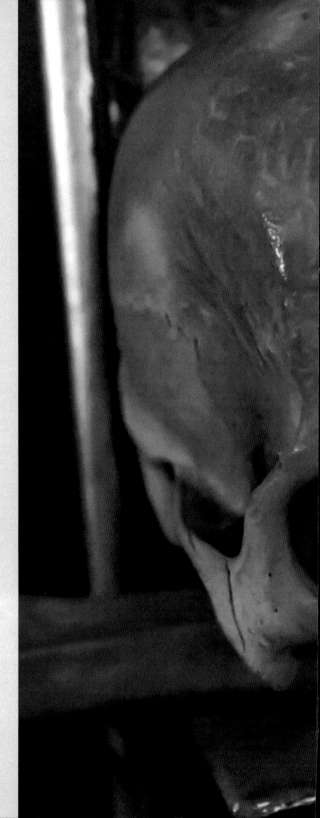

There is more to know about the black plague. Research and have fun!

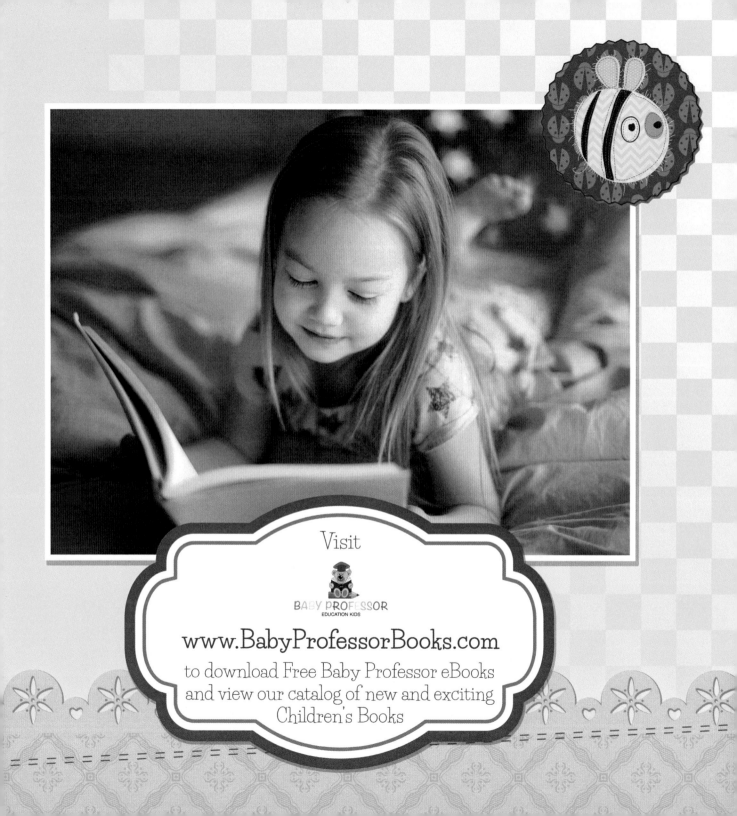

Visit

BABY PROFESSOR
EDUCATION KIDS

www.BabyProfessorBooks.com

to download Free Baby Professor eBooks
and view our catalog of new and exciting
Children's Books